The Music
HENRY MANCINI
Plus One

20 Great Songs To Play With Orchestral Accompaniment CD

Arranged by Tony Esposito
Background instruments performed and arranged by Andy Selby

CONTENTS

THE PINK PANTHER

By HENRY MANCINI
Arranged by TONY ESPOSITO

IF9723

MOON RIVER

Music by HENRY MANCINI
Arranged by TONY ESPOSITO

IF9723

MEGGIE'S THEME
(a/k/a "Anywhere the Heart Goes")

Music by HENRY MANCINI
Arranged by TONY ESPOSITO

IF9723

BABY ELEPHANT WALK

By HENRY MANCINI
Arranged by TONY ESPOSITO

IF9723

THE SWEETHEART TREE

Music by HENRY MANCINI
Arranged by TONY ESPOSITO

IF9723

BREAKFAST AT TIFFANY'S

By HENRY MANCINI
Arranged by TONY ESPOSITO

DAYS OF WINE AND ROSES

Music by HENRY MANCINI
Arranged by TONY ESPOSITO

SOFTLY

By HENRY MANCINI
Arranged by TONY ESPOSITO

Moderately slow

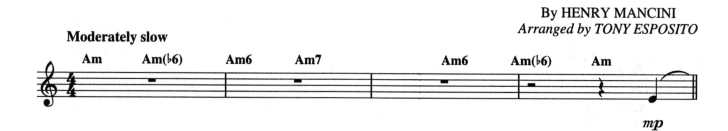

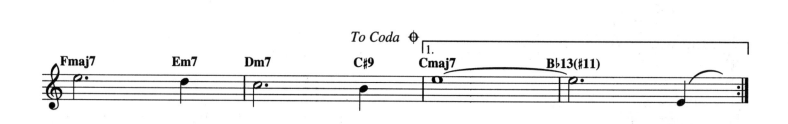

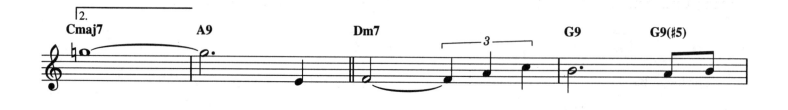

IF9723

BLACKIE'S TUNE
("The Man Who Loved Women")

By HENRY MANCINI
Arranged by TONY ESPOSITO

SLOW HOT WIND

Music by HENRY MANCINI
Arranged by TONY ESPOSITO

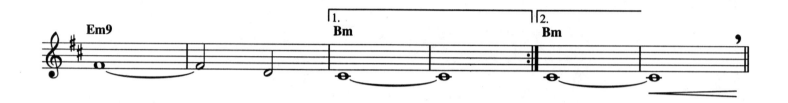

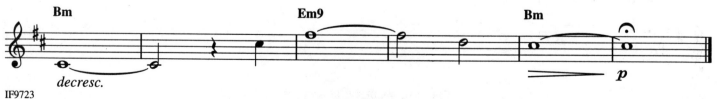

IF9723

PETER GUNN THEME

By HENRY MANCINI
Arranged by TONY ESPOSITO

© 1958 (Renewed 1986) NORTHRIDGE MUSIC COMPANY
All Rights Reserved

"LE JAZZ HOT!"

Music by HENRY MANCINI
Arranged by TONY ESPOSITO

IF9723

BRASS ON IVORY
Dedicated to DOC SEVERINSEN

By HENRY MANCINI
Arranged by TONY ESPOSITO

molto rit.

let fade

IF9723

CHARADE

Music by HENRY MANCINI
Arranged by TONY ESPOSITO

A COOL SHADE OF BLUE

By HENRY MANCINI
Arranged by TONY ESPOSITO

IF9723

MR. LUCKY

Music by HENRY MANCINI
Arranged by TONY ESPOSITO

IF9723

FLUTER'S BALL

By HENRY MANCINI
Arranged by TONY ESPOSITO

DREAMSVILLE

Music by HENRY MANCINI
Arranged by TONY ESPOSITO

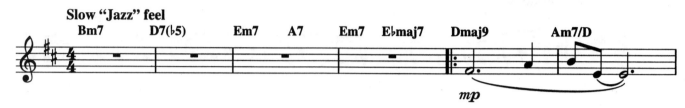

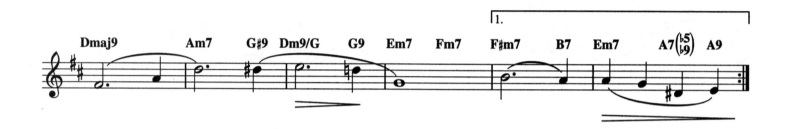

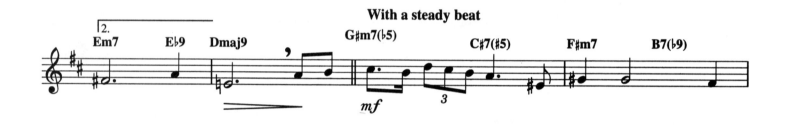

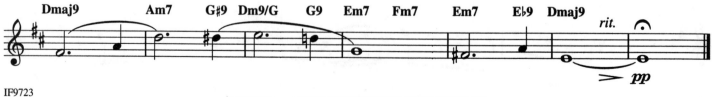

IF9723